David In

HINDRANCES TO FAITH

THINK   When our problems seem to be too big for us it is easy to despair. As we listen to the news and see all the sad things that happen, we can begin to doubt the love and power of God. Discouragement, despair, doubt. All these things are enemies of our faith.

PRAYER   Lord, show me how to fight the enemies of discouragement, despair and doubt. You have rescued me before and you will rescue me again.

READ   **1 Samuel 17:31–51.** David's faith could have been deterred by three things. First was the reaction of Eliab, his eldest brother (28). Scorn from those who know us best easily discourages us. David's second deterrent could have been his inability to wear Saul's armour (39). The uniform would have helped David to look impressive. Being unable to wear it might have made David think again. The third deterrent could have been the sarcastic words from Goliath (42–44).

But David was undeterred! His experience in the wilderness had taught him to be unafraid of enemies who were bigger and stronger than he was. He planned to use his tried and tested method, depending on the God who had never yet failed him (37,45).

CONSIDER *David, a man who depended on God; a man after God's heart.* David would never have risen to such heights of faith if he had not learnt to trust God in the smaller issues of each day.

REFLECT *'Fight the good fight with all thy might,*
Christ is thy strength, and Christ thy right
Faint not, nor fear, his arms are near
He changeth not, and thou art dear.'

                                                    J S B Mansell

Turn the verses of this hymn into a prayer of trust and confidence in God.

THE BIBLE IN A YEAR: JEREMIAH 51, 52: PSALM 119: 73–96

SEEING WITH FAITH

REFLECT   '"I know the plans that I have for you," says the Lord, "plans for welfare and not for evil, to give you a future and a hope"' (Jer 29:11 RSV).

PRAISE   Lord, I worship you.
You know what you want from me.
You know what you are doing with me.
Lord, I love you.

READ   **1 Samuel 17:17–30.** As far as David was concerned this was just another day. It wasn't the first time that he had gone to the battle lines to see how his brothers fared and to take food to them and their commanding officer. But God had other plans for David that day. Notice how the Israelite army react to Goliath (24). Then see how David reacts (26b,36,37).

The reason that David knew he could trust God when facing this giant of a man was because he had learnt to trust God day by day as he cared for his sheep. What are the things that you are needing to trust God for? Name these things to him. What past experiences can help you find new confidence today?

CONSIDER   As you face another day, how do you see it? Do you think that God's view of the new day is the same as yours? To look at a situation with the eye of faith is very different from looking at it with fear, or depression or anxiety.

THINK   You and God face each new day together.

PRAYER   Lord, thank you that whatever this new day holds, you and I are together. Help me to remember that you are with me. Help me to trust you with the things I have named before you.

Prayer Focus: Pray for SU Scotland's new General Director, Colin Sinclair, in his leadership responsibilities.

THE BIBLE IN A YEAR: JEREMIAH 49, 50: JOHN 18

A LATE LARK SINGING

John Kett

MINERVA PRESS
LONDON
MONTREUX   LOS ANGELES   SYDNEY

ISBN 1 75410 016 2

First Published 1997 by
MINERVA PRESS
195 Knightsbridge
London SW7 1RE

Printed in Great Britain for Minerva Press

A LATE LARK SINGING

To Mary with love

About the Author

John Kett has spent all his life, apart from the war years, in Norfolk, working as a teacher. Now retired, he lives in the village of Cawston, to which he came as a headmaster in 1952. His love of the natural world and his rural hobbies, including gardening and beekeeping, were shared with his wife, Mary, until her death in 1994. His affection for the country encouraged him to write several books of Norfolk verse, which have been popular since the 1970s. Many of his poems have been read on radio programmes. He has served as a Reader in churches in the locality since 1957, and much of his verse reflects this work. His family of five grandchildren and two married sons live nearby and keep him young at heart.

Note on the Title

The author was reading some of W.E. Henley's verse when this book was being prepared for publication, at a time when he was celebrating his eightieth birthday, and the fields of his native Norfolk were echoing to the singing of skylarks. The title comes from Henley's 'Margaritae Sorori', which includes the lines:

> My task accomplish'd and the long day done,
> My wages taken, and in my heart
> Some late lark singing...

Contents

A Simple Faith

I

Another day is dawning; comes the light;
Stars slowly fade, and steadily the sun
Ascends the sky, and touches one by one
With gold the lingering traces of the night.

Proceeding on its long-predestined way,
Precisely planned, goes little planet Earth.
Back in uncharted time, some cosmic birth
Began this cavalcade of night and day.

Of countless worlds, and many past our seeing,
This world's but one, and on through time and space
Speeds this great chariot of the human race,
This wondrous orb on which we have our being.

And being here, how do we fill the days
That constitute our lives, the months, the years?
Are we but slaves of our mundane careers,
Too busy to consider higher ways?

Perhaps, from time to time, we raise our eyes
Above our own affairs, the trivial scene;
But worldly worries swiftly intervene,
Visions are vanquished even as they rise.

And if by some rare chance there comes our way
A transitory gleam of mystic light,
We find ourselves bedazzled by the sight;
Our little minds withdraw in disarray.

II

The universe, and nature's history,
Our simple senses tell, are finely planned.
We see so much, so little understand;
The Planner still remains a mystery.

Who seeks for wisdom will do well to turn
To simple things, not reaching out too far.
Study a stone, and not a distant star,
If you would of the great Creator learn.

Study a stone; within may lie concealed
A dull, hard core, or crystals sparkling bright,
And he who breaks the pebble brings to light
A secret through the ages unrevealed.

The workmanship we see throughout creation
Bespeaks a master-craftsman; all we find
Is evidence of some great mastermind,
Of power and purpose too, a demonstration.

III

A daisy grows; white petals cluster round
The golden disc that smiles towards the sun.
The daisy dies, but unseen rootlets run,
And other daisies rise above the ground.

A caterpillar to a nettle clings,
It eats the leaves, and grows, then hangs concealed.
A few weeks pass; its glory is revealed;
A butterfly glides by on gorgeous wings.

A young lark flutters falteringly along.
The soft wings gather strength, and soaring high,
And higher still, its praises fill the sky,
Carefree cascades of sweet, primeval song.

A snowflake falls, and melts, and through the earth
It sinks to find a stream, thence to the sea,
Then in a wondrous way it rises free
To join the clouds above and find rebirth.

A great wave breaks in splendour on the shore,
With white foam flying, and with life abounding.
Far up the beach it leaps, the pebbles pounding,
Filling the air around with thunderous roar.

IV

As in the sea-spray every droplet tells
The nature of the ocean whence it springs,
So the life force pervades all living things,
So the Creator in each creature dwells.

It is as if in every soul a light,
A part of greater Light, is ever burning.
We are aware of it, without discerning
Its source, or guide, or goal, however bright.

This greater Light, Creator, Planner, Mind,
Men call Great Spirit, Allah, God, or Brahma,
As down the years through time's long panorama
The search for truth continues for mankind.

We see the evidence that God is here,
And there, and everywhere, yet yearn to know
More of His nature. There's so much to show
That He indeed exists, but does He care?

V

A baby's born; the mother's love surrounds
The tiny being, strengthens as it grows;
And from our dear ones, love about us flows;
A searching, gentle tide that knows no bounds.

If human life with love is permeated,
And we for one another deeply care,
Surely God loves; if not, it would appear
He stands below the beings He created.

The finest qualities that man possesses
Are surely in his Maker, and indeed,
Believing this may well be what we need
To rise above our wonderings and our guesses.

But if He cares for us, how can it be
That suffering so often comes our way?
Sickness or sadness mar the brightest day;
Faith falters in the midst of misery.

As children do their parents' laws reject,
And do not see their worth till later years,
So in perspective all our griefs and fears
May show in better light, in retrospect.

VI

But whence come we, and whither are we bound?
Have we been here before? Will we return?
So much we wish to know, and long to learn
Where answers to our questions may be found.

Do other worlds lie far beyond our knowing?
Are very different beings living there?
Do Sons of God from time to time appear,
On them their words of hope and love bestowing?

Such knowledge lies with God, in His perfection;
To know that He is with us, ever caring,
Provides a path to follow, without fearing.
More tortuous ways may make us lose direction.

God's canvas spreads too far for human eyes
The whole of His creation to survey;
That little part of it we see each day
The signs of its magnificence supplies.

The path leads onwards through this glorious setting
In which we find ourselves, where time and tide
Bring many changes, and we need a guide
To help us on our way, with no regretting.

The circumstances of our birth affect
The pattern of our spiritual ways.
In church, or mosque, or temple we give praise,
And in our forebears' faith our course direct.

And so it is that guidance comes in sight
In many forms. From farthest east to west,
We seek the way that seems for us the best,
With common goal, but varied leading light.

VII

To Christians comes the call sublime and clear;
'I am the Way,' says Jesus, 'follow me!'
Directly and with sweet simplicity,
The invitation comes for all to hear.

He stands prepared to lead us day by day,
Past all the sad distractions that abound
Along the road, and in His words are found
All the advice we need upon life's way.

Another day is dawning, with the treasure
Of glorious sunlight, but a wealth untold
Comes from the Inner Light for those who hold
A Simple Faith, a blessing beyond measure.

1987

Space Mission

Half in wonder, half in fear,
The young man stayed, to stand and stare
As the thunder rolled away
From the hill, across the bay.
For there before him on the beach lay still
The shining shape that he, upon the hill,
Had seen descending from the stormy skies.
Spellbound, he stared, as there appeared
A movement in the glow before his eyes.
Then as he watched, as he indeed expected,
A ladder slowly lowered, he detected.
And while upon surrounding rocks
The pounding breakers surged,
A figure down the ladder came,
And from the craft emerged
To face the sea, and standing straight and tall,
Stretched out a steady hand, as if in reprimand,
And peace pervaded all.
The gale died down, and faded right away;
Tranquillity returned across the bay.

The watcher turned; within he burned
With desperate desire to run,
To hurry down into the town,
To tell his tale to everyone.
The way to leave the spot he quickly planned;
He took a step, then stopped; he felt a hand

Rest firmly on his arm.
He felt no fear, but rather was surprised,
And in that very moment realised
That he was free from harm.

A voice he heard, such lovely tones
Unheard on Earth before,
And yet their meaning clearly came
To him. Indeed, far more,
He felt that he was standing face to face,
Not with a stranger come from distant space,
But with a trusted friend, on whom he could depend.

And so it was he found himself inside
The craft upon the beach. He met the crew,
And gradually the feeling in him grew
Of mutual love and trust All fear had died.
So much they wished to know; so much he told
About our life on Earth; and growing bold,
He spoke of evil things, of crime, starvation,
Of nation waging bitter war with nation;
Disturbing fears, distressing cares,
So often the result of human failing;
The troubles men create with selfishness and hate,
The hopelessness and helplessness prevailing.
And as the sorry story was expanding,
His listeners slowly nodded, understanding.

At last he tired. It seemed he'd told them all,
And through the window in the crystal wall
He saw that night had come. For many hours
He had talked on, encouraged by their powers.
And then it was the one who met him first
Took both his hands, and gazed into his eyes.
'We came', he said, 'to satisfy our thirst
For knowledge of your Earth. We realise
The faith that is our pride to you has been denied.
For to our people, long ago,
Came one who lived a life
That clearly to us all did show
The foolishness of strife.
He was Divine. Through Him did shine
One law, all laws above;
A rule sublime, for endless time,
The Golden Rule of Love.'

The speaker paused, and for a moment
seemed so far away.
A little smile came to his face,
and he went on to say,
'It's time for us to leave.
Farewell, and do not grieve
If men will not believe the news you give.
We shall return one day,
And help you all, I pray,
To live such lives as we have learned to live.'

The young man clambered down upon the sand.
The door behind him closed; he saw a hand

Wave from the window where his friend,
still smiling, now was standing.
And then the vessel slowly rose,

as he had seen it landing.
'Twas then the waving figure
cast his crimson cloak aside;
'Twas then the wondering watcher
on the moonlit beach espied
Suspended from the traveller's neck,
confirming all he'd told,
Upon a fine and glittering chain
A Crucifix of gold.

Now they were gone; he saw the craft no more,
But stayed alone upon the silent shore
Until the sky grew light,
And ended the long night.
And while the pale moon in the west
was slowly, slowly sinking,
A man stood quietly praying there,
and thinking, deeply thinking.

1967

Just a Minute

The bells hang silent in the old clock tower,
Rising high above the town,
And a full moon shines on the streets below,
Where a thousand people come and go
From a thousand private heavens and hells,
In the shadow of the tower with the silent bells.
But just one sound in the tower is found,
Steadily repeated as the wheels go round,
Far above the clamour of the busy street,
The heavy and unhurried, regular beat
Of the slow, solemn seconds, measuring the time,
Creeping towards the moment of the glorious chime.

The two great hands now mark the hour
Of nine. The great clock gathers power,
And now to life the bells are springing,
Their clear notes round the town are ringing.
The clock tower echoes with the sounds,
From wall to wall the peal rebounds.
This lively introduction past,
The hour starts striking, and at last,
In measured majesty sublime,
The great clock tells the town the time.

Below upon the pavement crowds pass by,
But only one man upward casts an eye.
He checks his watch, then goes upon his way

To tell his family of his busy day.
One minute's passed since first the bells were stirred,
And now once more the steady rhythm's heard.
Along time's stream have sixty seconds gone,
And still the ticking of the clock goes on.

Within that measured minute, near at hand,
With every action timed, rehearsed, and planned,
A robber crouches, peering at a lock
In a safe door within an office block.
His practised fingers travel here and there
Across the shining steel, his ready ear
Alert for every movement, and his eyes
Are sharply focused where a torch supplies
A tiny beam of light. His forehead glistens
As, holding breath, he bends his head and listens.
A final click, and as the minute ends,
The door swings open and an arm extends
Within the safe. And now a robber stands
With others' hard-earned money in his hands.

Meanwhile at that same time, a mile away,
Another expert has his part to play
With nimble fingers: life is in his hands.
With white-clad figures near, a surgeon stands,
Gloved, masked, alert; voice low and curt.
Decision... and incision, with infinite precision.
The task has but begun, and much is to be done.

The little team's committed; their leader, so well fitted
With skill and knowledge, knows that all goes well,
As the ninth stroke sounds from the distant bell.

An island far away... a shadow falls
Upon a burning strand, a crescent of white sand,
The shadow of a lonely, lofty palm
Which stands in isolation, midst the charm
The blue Pacific breeds. The shadow crawls
So slowly on the sand, as mounts the sun
His daily course to run.
No living creature stirs, for few are here.
There's motion in the waves, but that is all;
Here time is only told as shadows crawl.
No one is here to measure each minute, or to treasure
The joy of time set free beside this timeless sea.

But while the shadow creeps on that far shore,
Within an eastern city moves a maze
Of countless beings on their various ways,
Through dingy shop and busy little store;
Babbling tongues, street vendors hailing,
Swinging signs, and beggars wailing,
Hurrying, worrying, coming, going,
About their business, scarcely knowing
What's happening within the minute,
So much activity is in it.
Yet each within his little world is living,
With scarce a thought to others ever giving,
As everywhere they flow and flock and throng,
Upon the tide of turmoil borne along.

In sweltering office, plied with cooling drinks,
A plump, perspiring man is scheming out a plan.
He nods his head and doodles as he thinks,
Picks up a telephone, speaks slowly, puts it down,
Then chuckles, sips, and sits back at his ease...
He's made another fortune in rupees.
Outside the city, on a stony waste,
A weary ploughman pauses at his toil,
And sadly gazes at the sun-baked soil.
He shakes his head; his oxen patient stand;
The heat-haze shimmers on the burning land.

An old man sits beneath a tree,
Alone upon a mountainside;
Below him deep, dark waters glide:
A sacred stream that searches for the sea.
Silent he sits, and gazes far
Beyond the moonlit, snow-tipped height,
As if to penetrate the night,
And see beyond the farthest, gleaming star.
For years he's stared beyond those peaks,
In silence there; he does not know
When someone will eventually show
His contemplating soul the truth he seeks.

For worldly fears and loves and hates
He cares not, feeling time will bring
A voice revealing everything,
A million minutes, or but one, he waits...

Others with anxious faces raise their eyes
To see a glowing object climb the skies,
Not waiting for an unknown voice,
In lengthy silence; they rejoice
To see their work succeed, as now apace
Their task of months goes soaring into space.
They're counting here in seconds, even less,
For timing is the essence of success.
And yet the hillside mystic, distant far,
Knows naught of this, sees but a tiny star.

And thus throughout the world each part is played.
The little lives are lived, and plans are made
By people who can never surely know
What the next minute holds. Some come, some go;
A baby's born; an old man dies;
A gay girl laughs; a poor child cries.
Kings rule, dictators rant, and beggars wail;
One fails to learn, another learns to fail.
A traveller departs, and one arrives;
The unexpected touches many lives.
And thus does life go on, and one more minute's gone.

All this and more within a planet small,
And more besides, for none can know it all.
And as the minutes pass, far out in space
The universe maintains its breathless pace.
New galaxies appear, whirl on their way
In fiery glory, and this great display
Each second is expanding beyond our understanding,
Creating an illusion that all is in confusion.

Yet all is nicely planned,
As if some mighty hand
Held every part in place
Controlling it in space,
And guiding every movement far and near,
Precisely and with calculated care.
Throughout vast realms of space, beyond imagination,
Throughout all time's expanse, unfailing since creation.

The old man stirs beneath the tree.
Alone upon the mountainside.
Upon the troubled world he gazes down,
Then scans the heavens with a puzzled frown.
With such a well-controlled and careful plan,
Can there be chaos in the world of man?
Slowly he rises; little does he know,
But much believes; the skies around him show
The power that is there.
He stands in silent prayer,
As if to reach that great controlling hand,
Contented, though he fails to understand...

And far away another man looks down
Above the rooftops of a busy town,
A wizened little man, so quiet and meek,
Who carefully performs his task each week.
Just after nine, he slowly turns the lock,
Enters the clock tower, and winds up the clock...

The Months

January Snow

Silently came the snow before the dawn,
And in the countryside new beauty's born.
We see around us on this glittering morn
New wonders now revealed. Small footprints show
Where birds and tiny, hungry creatures go;
Gulls, white against the sky, come swooping low,
And turn against the dazzling field to grey.
The sunbeams dancing on the snow convey
A brightness even to the sombre pines,
And where a leaf breaks through the snow it shines
With brilliance that is usually unseen
At times when all around is brown or green.
Deep winter's here, but though chill winds may blow
They bring to us the glory of the snow.

February Promise

In sheltered spots the colours now return.
Brave crocuses and aconites of gold
Form brilliant carpets on the dreary floor
Of winter borders. In the woods unfold
The spikes of cuckoo pint, now showing more
And brighter green than hardy fronds of fern.
There's colour, too, where tits and finches fly,
Attired already for the affairs of spring.
And, welcome even more, on oak branch high
As daylight fades a thrush begins to sing.
The hazel catkins shiver in the breeze,
In yellow clouds pale pollen drifts away.
A thousand starlings pass above the trees,
And silvered silk the willow wands display.

March Birth

The lively breezes fleecy flocks are chasing
Across the sky; from field to field go racing
Cloud shadows, hurrying on beneath the sun.
On every side man's work is being done,
To profit by this time when all around
The life renewed is springing from the ground.
Dawn's chorus swells; at dusk the blackthorn's glowing,
Hedges grow green, and chattering children stray
Along the banks where primroses are growing
With daffodils. And on this first warm day
A butterfly with sunlit, yellow wings
Goes gaily gliding by; a robin sings,
And celandines among the mosses gleam,
Casting their gold upon the busy stream.

April Growth

A soft wind stirs a ripple on the lake;
A water-hen calls once, then hides away.
The silver birch tree's branches gently sway,
And on the water gay reflections make
Of merry multitudes of dancing leaves
Which rustle in the wind. And now on high
A single swallow from the south soars by.
Beside the woodland's edge the warm earth heaves
With new life bursting forth. Each bush and tree
Now greener grows, as if with real desire
To help the nesting birds, and to conspire
With them to make concealment quite complete,
While waves of rippling song are flowing free
From skylarks rising from the growing wheat.

May Colour

The bright and busy days of May are here;
The countryside's ablaze with colours rare
In sun and shower. There's cricket on the green,
And lilies in the wood, and now are seen
Laburnums pouring gold, tall chestnuts decked
With spires of pink and white, where bees collect
A precious harvest, then away go winging
Past lovely lilacs where a blackbird's singing.
Old gardeners now their long experience bring
To battle with the weeds; the lawns are neat.
A worried thrush scolds by the garden seat
Her wandering, gaping brood. House-martins cling,
Pied master-builders, on the weathered walls,
And from the woods all day the cuckoo calls.

June Light

Late lingers now the light, and through the night
A glow creeps eastward round the northern sky.
The sun comes early, quickly rises high,
Shines down upon a world of June delight;
On fields of hay, and lanes where grasses sway,
Their graceful panicles in fine array.
Wild roses, soft of hue, and fragrant briar,
And wayside wastes with poppies set afire.
Now family parties picnic by the stream,
Or roam in wonder under mighty trees,
And little children plough through bracken seas,
Wild fancies flying in a waking dream.
At last dusk falls, and shadowy moths appear
Where honeysuckle scents the evening air.

July Storm

The towering clouds recede; the storm has fled;
The dark and angry sky grows clear again.
The thunder faintly rolls, and slowly dies,
And skylarks twitter gladly as they rise.
Now many a flower hangs low a dripping head,
And here and there a patch of levelled grain
Recalls the violence of the summer storm.
The sun returns, the rain-soaked earth grows warm.
Slow and ungainly by the waterside
A solemn toad plods forth, and small snails glide,
Their shining shells enriched by golden rings.
A dragon-fly with wide and wondrous wings
Glows like a jewel there among the reeds,
Above the tangle of the water-weeds.

August Afternoon

Suddenly now we see the cornfields white,
Ready for harvest, while the summer sun
Shines down with welcome warmth, its brilliant light
Making the heat-haze dance, as one by one
The humming harvesters crawl 'cross the fields,
And once again good grain the good earth yields.
The roads are busy with the hurrying horde
Of folks on holiday; the heavens are clear
And blue, so very blue, with their reward
For those who have the time to stand and stare.
For there young swallows mount into the sky,
And thistledown upon the breeze dreams by.
Grasshoppers chirr, and where the creeper clings
A peacock butterfly outspreads its wings.

September Morning

September morning, with the warm sun growing
In warmth and brightness, scattering mists of pearl,
Which round the waking village flow and furl.
And see, the top of the church tower is glowing,
Splendid, sunlit, above the misty sea,
Now ebbing fast to set the morning free.
Along the hedgerow countless dying weeds
Show one last beauty in their feathered seeds.
The chattering sparrows wheel, and wheel again
Across the stubble field, and by the lane,
Among the dew-drenched grasses hardly seen,
Yet showing rarely a sun-gilded sheen,
A silver maze of gossamer is spread,
While all around hang berries, richly red.

October Evening

Today it rained; across the evening sky
Grey, ragged ranks of cloud now slowly pass
After the rain away, and out to sea.
We near the old wood; from a dripping tree
Leaves, damp and yellow, fall upon the grass,
As startled pigeons from their cover fly.
A pheasant calls; gnats dance by ivy blooms;
Among the bracken blood-red brambles run.
The daylight fades, and in the scattered homes
The little windows light up one by one.
In cottage gardens now the beacons glow
Of white chrysanthemums, defying night;
Pale, cold, the moon glides slowly into sight,
And trees across the fields faint shadows throw.

November Night

Dull dawn, grey day, and early comes the night,
Now wearisome November's here again,
With frost to follow frost, then chilling rain,
Or fog comes stealthily, and hides from sight
The dripping world beyond the window pane.
But oh, the glory when the night is clear,
What glittering feast for eyes that scan the skies!
See Jupiter near old Orion rise,
The Bear, the Bull, and Pegasus appear,
And see, a meteor falls, and glows, and dies.
Nearby an owl is calling; now it flies
On silent, velvet wings, while all grows cold.
Frost's icy fingers woods and fields enfold,
And touch with silver lingering leaves of gold.

December Day

This shortest day of all the year was born
When fiery cloud-banks filled the eastern sky.
Concealed in grey since that belated dawn
The sun remains, and all around rise high
The latticed traceries of sleeping trees.
Beneath them now the woodland wanderer sees
So little living, little colour too,
For winter's dull, damp blanket hides from view
The fallen glory of the year grown old,
And future beauty waiting to unfold.
And so to Christmas, festival of light,
When families in joy and hope unite,
To celebrate the birthday all remember,
Bringing a blaze of brightness to December.

Fingal's Cave

Can any words be woven to achieve
Description worthy of the wonder here?
For only those who see it can conceive
The stately splendour of the rocks that rise
In great, majestic columns towards the skies,
And high above a patterned ceiling bear,
With mottled beauty in mosaic rare.

Beneath this mighty arch deep waters flow,
And all the ocean's mystery convey,
For here are pleasing sounds that come and go,
As, searching onwards, each succeeding wave
Explores the farthest reaches of the cave,
Breaks on the rocks, its little part to play,
And then returns upon its endless way.

A sense of power divine this cavern fills,
And peace nearby Iona quietly shares,
That everlasting quality the hills
Display on misty islands all around.
Here time becomes eternity profound,
And in perspective are the passing years...
Here is God's work, remote, sublime, and free,
A glorious harmony of rocks and sea...

1967

Iceland

This strange, romantic land, this Iceland...
Land of ice mountains, lava plains, black sand,
Fountains of steam, great waterfalls that gleam
And glitter in the sun, and rocks that seem
To tremble as we walk. Here flames may rise
Out of the hills towards the northern skies.
This far-off, friendly land, this Iceland...
Where flowers like jewels are blooming where we stand,
Watching the swift sea-swallows wheel and soar,
Where for the wandering traveller every door
Offers a welcome. Here the air is sweet,
The water tastes like wine, and those we meet
Convey a warmth, a friendliness sincere...
All this, and more, awaits the stranger there.

Reykjavik, 1985

The Simmer Din

Midnight has come, and the skies are clear
On this, the shortest night of the year.
We see from our window the waves below
In the reflected, golden glow,
That gentle light of the simmer dim,
As the sun steals eastward below the rim
Of the Shetland hills, with their carpet of flowers
Scenting the air through the summer hours.
High overhead the white gulls wheel,
Rising and falling, as if they feel
Pleasure at gliding the hours away,
Awaiting the warmth of the sun's first ray.
In peaceful silence their joy we share
On this, the shortest night of the year.

Lerwick, 1986

Ski-Lift at Grindelwald

Surrounded by splendour, by breathtaking beauty,
Aloft in the ski-lift, side by side,
Above and away from the colourful carpet
Of Grindelwald's rooftops together we glide.

Silently sailing we pass over pastures
With wild flowers bejewelled, and clusters of trees
Raising their branches to wave far below us,
Starred by the sunbeams and stirred by the breeze.

Cowbells ring sweetly to break the deep silence,
Fading away in the valley below,
As upward we climb, and we feel icy fingers
Touching our cheeks as we come to the snow.

At last on the white-mantled slope we're alighting,
Great mountains around us, majestic and clear.
Surpassing the splendour, the breathtaking beauty,
The power and the glory surrounded us there.

Switzerland, 1982

43

Peat Fire

We gazed at the glow, and talked of familiar things
As together we sat that night by a fire of peat,
The collie, her head on her paws, asleep at our feet;
And our thoughts took wings.

Outside, the heather and cotton-grass covered the hill,
And away to the north was a mirror of sea for miles.
The evening was bringing its peace to the lovely isles,
But the air was chill.

For the year had turned, and we welcomed the cheerful heat;
Life's fast pace eased, and time for a while stood still.
And we'll long remember that night, the heather, the hill...
And the glow of the peat.

John o'Groats, 1967

Leningrad in Spring

Through old St Petersburg the river glides,
The slow, sun-stippled Neva, now ice-free
Since welcome spring has spread across the plain,
Warming the earth, and greening every tree,
To reach this Venice of the north again.

Along the banks old men lean on low walls,
Grey-clad, bemedalled, watching memories pass;
And sturdy girls in trousers work away,
Paint the park seats, and sweep, and cut the grass,
Unsmiling on this lovely day in May.

In slow procession little children walk
On pilgrimage political, with flowers;
While guided tourists view the treasure store
Displayed beneath the city's gilded towers,
And see Great Peter ride his steed ashore.

Leningrad, 1983

45

Bateau Mouche

A summer evening, and flies at the window,
Reminding me once again
Of a summer night on a 'bateau mouche'
With you on the River Seine.
An evening of shadows that came and went
As bridges passed slowly by,
With the lights of Paris dimming the stars
That powdered the cloudless sky.

Lovers lingered by darkened walls
As we gently drifted past
On the shining waters that swirled and curled
Until we saw at last
The floodlit spire of Notre Dame,
Its buttresses and its towers,
Crowning the pleasure we shared that night
On the Seine in those magical hours.

Paris, 1981

To Arran in Autumn

When autumn comes, we'll go again to Arran,
Leave Brodick Pier, and take the road uphill,
Then eastward tramp across the fading heather
To look out from Dun Finn. All will be still
Except the twittering birds among the bracken,
Which will, we know, be glowing red and gold.
The sea will seem to sleep, all sunshine-silvered;
The Holy Isle will rest there, as of old,
Peacefully lying, like an anchored galleon,
Shelt'ring the shores of lovely Lamlash Bay...
Then we'll go down among the hazel bushes,
Laden with nuts, leaves falling. Now the day
Is dying; we must chase the last rays westward,
And head across the Ross; see sunset's glow.
Weary, we'll rest, drink in the island's beauty...
When autumn comes, to Arran we will go...

September 1960

47

To Mary, on Holy Isle

The rolling tide is filling the bay,
The hills are touched by the sun's last ray;
Nothing moves in the cloudless sky
But a white gull gliding by.

Surrounded by beauty on land and sea,
I feel you are sharing it all with me,
Seeing the signs of God's peace and power,
Sharing this evening hour.

Here in the calm of this Holy Isle,
Aware of your love, your voice, your smile;
Here in the silence I feel you near.
Unseen, you are with me, dear...

Lindisfarne, 1996

Holy Evening

The westering sun, the call of a gull,
The murmur of bees.

The sound of a psalm, a whisper of prayer,
The breeze in the trees.

Memories of walking the shores and the meadows,
And facing the weather.

And now through this evening our spirits in silence
Wander together.

Lindisfarne, 1996

Indian Nightfall

The new moon, queen of night, reigns in the sky,
Where minutes before a blazing sun held sway.
Suddenly, darkness out of the east comes nigh,
Chasing the westward traces of the day.
But though the sun is gone, the light dispersed,
The heat still lingers, and the desert's thirst

Monotonously the evening cricket sings,
And from the village faintly now I hear
An Indian song, an eerie chant that brings
Out of the shadows on the heavy air
A sense of mystery, a note of warning,
Which will remain until the glow of morning.

Mercilessly, a hot, dust-laden breeze
Swirls past, as if to chase the exhausted day,
Rattling those skeletons of dry, old trees,
Then disappearing in the deepening grey.
A whisper grows; things stir; and unseen wings
Pass by me; night is here; the cricket sings.

Sialkot, 1946

50

Touch of Summer

Soft streams of cirrus cloud flow down the sky,
Far overhead, miles high,

So soft, so far away;
While near to us, so near,
A bracken frond bends low to touch your hair.

Cawston Heath, 1968

51

Enrichment in Spring

I've seen it all before: the longed-for greening
Of hedgerows in the early days of May;
The bursting buds on trees across the way;
The first blue speedwells; dandelions of gold;
The bracken fronds that from the earth unfold,
The mossy banks from warmer sunlight screening;
The sudden show of speckled arum leaves;
The soaring swallow as above it weaves...
I've seen it all before, and sought its meaning.

I've heard, year after year, the cuckoo singing,
Unseen within the wood, a call so clear,
Above the rippling song, a joy to hear,
Of skylarks rising high. And listen, now
A song thrush pours his poetry from the bough,
From yonder chestnut tree his joy is springing.
I've heard before the laughter of the brooks,
Cry of the moorhen, cawing of the rooks
Above their lofty homes at sunset winging.

And I have felt before the passing breeze,
The gentle touch of warm, soft-falling rain,
The new-dug earth, and all along the lane
Caress of graceful grasses grown so tall;
The sun-warmed flints that top the garden wall;
The cooling shade beneath the apple trees.
And as the hives reveal their growing store
I gently move my hand within once more,
To feel the velvet clinging of the bees.

Why are they all enriched today, and clearer,
These things I've heard, and seen, and felt before?
It could, of course, be simply that once more
The days are lengthening as they've warmer grown
After the coldest winter we have known.
No, more than this makes all these wonders dearer.
Advancing years, it seems, are now endowing
With fuller meaning all that nature's showing,
As God, through His Creation, draws me nearer.

1979

St Peter's Church, Haveringland

'Lift up your eyes,' said Jesus,
'And look on the fields, to learn.'[1]
And here, in Haver'land's fields today,
We also, in our turn,
Witness the pageant of seasons,
The ever-changing scene,
Which, as men work along with God,
Turns gold, or brown, or green.

Let us remember our forebears,
Who in the years gone by
Surveyed a scene so different,
Yet under the same great sky.
The days of the abbey, the market,
The hall and the airfield pass
Each down the road of history,
Now rubble under the grass.

Wars and rumours of wars have come
And gone, like the stately trees,
And now where the noisy engines roared
We hear the hum of the bees.
We live in a world of changes,
Yet surely the lesson is clear;
Amidst it all, as on a rock,
St Peter's Church stands here,

---

[1]   John 4:35

Symbol of truths that never change,
Of a faith that never yields,
And we find the eternal peace of God
In His Church among the fields.

1960

Church Festival

Angel to angel calls,
'What music do we hear?'
Melody gently falls
Soft on the ear.
Delicate echoes flow out of the nave
Into the transepts, sweet wave upon wave.
See, where the music springs,
Silver head bowing low
Over the harp strings,
Where nimble fingers go.
Filling this beautiful church with a prayer,
Expressed not in words, but in music so clear.

Angel to angel calls,
'What wondrous scents are these,
Rising within these walls,
Borne on the breeze?'
They come from the flowers in their colourful splendour,
Which summertime gardens have had to surrender.

See how the roses glow,
Gracing the oaken pews;
Lilies and pansies show
Varied and blended hues;
Stately delphiniums, daisies so lowly,
Delicate foliage, and bold gladioli.

Angel to angel calls,
'What do we see below,
There where the sunlight falls,
Row upon row?'
Skills of past ages on canvas and leather,
Parchments and silver, all gathered together;
Wagon and resting plough,
No more to till;
Weaving loom, silent now;
Spinning wheel still.
Symbols of craftsmanship from bygone days,
Each representing a changing of ways.

Angel to angel calls,
'What do we feel,
Here in our lofty stalls?
Does this reveal
Simply desire on a stage to portray
Agnes, our saint, amid all this display?'
No, here is merit,
That surely now gleams
Some of the spirit
That raised these great beams.
Angel to angel calls, 'All then is well!'
See the last people leave, hear the church bell
Marking the end of the festival hours...
Imprisoned in splendour, bees visit the flowers.

Cawston, 1966

The Rood Screen at Cawston Church

How many hands achieved this stately beauty?
How many were the minds that pondered here?
The trees were felled, the various timbers fashioned,
Each panel, every arch, designed with care,
Each joint well fitted, every part perfected,
Then all, with Holy Rood above, erected.

Then came the artists of another kind,
With ochre, dragon's blood, fine shades of green,
And other worthy colours; with their skill
And careful hands they added to this screen
A glorious bequest for many ages,
Like a great book with ever-open pages.

And all the hands that left such beauty here
Can seem as two, together held in prayer;
The many minds whose visions here remain
As one mind seeking God, and not in vain.

1964

Tropical Shell

I hold within my hand the changing shades
Of countless colours from Pacific skies,
The smoothness of the calmest summer seas,
The perfect curve of gliding gull that flies
Above the shores of some far-distant land...
So beautiful, and held within my hand.

1971

North Sea Wave

Stormy days have come and gone,
But their anger grumbles on.
See that mighty wave advancing,
Terrifying, yet entrancing
Rushing towards us, ever growing,
From its crest white foam a-blowing,
Till at last with roar like thunder
At our feet it bursts asunder,
And the greedy waters reach farther up the battered beach.

Now the wind-whipped surf recedes,
Dragging stones and sand and weeds,
Sucking back the shifting shingle
Where the darker waters mingle
With the white and green and brown
Where the shore shelves sharply down.
See that watery cavern growing,
Filling, foaming, overflowing.
As with a rumble and a roar another wave dies on the shore.

Weybourne, 1967

Winter Walk

Frost on the window, robin on the sill,
The sun coming up in a clear, blue sky;
With time to spare on a day so fair
We walked to the heath, my love and I.

Ice on the puddles, frost-dried paths,
Tits a-twitter in the birch trees bright;
Cones on the pines, flowers on the gorse,
Green moss glowing in the wintry light.

Fieldfares flock on the frost-flecked fields,
The sun sinks slowly in the golden sky;
With thanks for the beauty this day revealed
We walked from the heath, my love and I.

Boxing Day, 1966

People in a Newmarket Cafe

Two lively little ladies chatter low,
Eyes wide and noses near,
While, munching biscuits as they older grow,
The aged couple stare.
The woman in the white hat sits and purrs,
Her friend growls in reply.
The solemn padre ponders, slowly stirs
His coffee, gives a sigh.
The little waitress with her tray flits past,
Bespectacled and fair;
Her taller partner, sad-faced, now at last
Writes out my bill, draws near.
I rise and pay, and say a silent grace
In thanks for coffee, and the human race.

1966

Blickling Woods in Autumn

A day of golden leaves, in thousands falling,
Of whispering breezes passing with a sigh;
Of flocks of pigeons, and of plovers calling,
And overhead a softly dappled sky.

Slow-flowing waters through the meadows run,
Then on into the woods, their sweet way wending;
A pair of swans, and in the west the sun,
And all that multitude of leaves descending...

1973

The Beekeeper

Two rows of hives within a sheltered glen;
We climbed the wayside bank to see them there.
The busy sound of countless hurrying bees
Came to our ears. It filled the August air
Beside the burn where we had stopped awhile.
Then came to us across the sloping lawn
The keeper of the bees, a shepherd too,
With brown and kindly face, and weather-worn,
Not hurrying, as if he'd naught to do
And all of time to do it. Speaking then
Of bees, his flock, his family, and the birds;
Showed us the hidden nest of tiny wren;
Spoke of the flowers, the sun, the welcome showers
Unhurriedly, he had so much to say;
What pity that we had no time to stay!
And so we left him with his bees, his flock,
As much of Arran as the very rock.

Isle of Arran, 1959

The Artist

The artist by the river stays his hand
To search his palette for elusive shades,
Striving to seize the sunlight ere it fades,
Preserving it and all this lovely land
Beside the glittering water. Does he find
The quest for colours easier than for me,
The quest for words? And is that bold beech tree
A challenge to his brush, as to my mind,
Which wrestles now with many a varied phrase,
Attempting to enfold the burnished leaves
Sun-flecked above us, where the swallow weaves?
His canvas nearly covered now I see,
So with the sun, the river, and the tree
In colour, and in words, we go our ways.

Coltishall, Norfolk, 1966

65

Cheese and Whine

The lawn's like velvet in the evening sun.
Across the well-trimmed grass long shadows run
Of people standing talking, by the roses,
People with cheese and wine, and sunburnt noses.
Their lively conversation fills the air,
And now and then across the lawn sounds clear
Above the song of birds, the chink of glasses
That tinkle on a tray as someone passes
Among the guests, ensuring that each one
Has wine to sparkle in the setting sun.
The low rays make the red wine even redder,
And touch with gold the Stilton and the Cheddar.
The tide of conversation ebbs and flows,
With talk of travels; how the garden grows;
Of schooling, and the question of selection;
And what the country needs; the next election.
While over there, with still determined jaws,
Three military men compare their wars...
But what's amiss? The vicar's wife is scratching
Her short-sleeved arm; the doctor's after catching
Some unseen thing behind his good wife's ear,
Only to lose it in her greying hair;
And see, our worthy and esteemed JP
Appears to have some trouble with his knee.

Now chaos reigns. The party, in a flurry,
In twos and threes, and trying not to hurry,
All go indoors, and eye the lawn askance,
Where half a million midges hold their dance.

1976

An Old-Fashioned Husband

Resplendent rooster, blood-red head held high;
Splendid your plumes as proudly you pass by!
Your brilliant eyes flash sharply all around
To cover your domain wherein are found
Your happy hens, that scratch among the weeds,
Searching contentedly for random seeds.
Their feathers indicate an age now fled,
Light Sussex here, and there Rhode Island Red,
And that attractive madam, like as not,
May well be called a fair White Wyandotte...
Well-fed and healthy, here your happy wives
Surround you, living out their little lives,
Old-fashioned in their ways as in their feathers.
They roam the fields and farmyard in all weathers,
Reminding passers-by with old-world charm
Of happier days before the battery farm.

Isle of Skye, 1972

'God Speed the Plough'

Across the clearing, with a pointed stake,
Man scratched first furrows
Over the new-won land; essayed to make
First fields. Slowly he learned.

Along straight strips, termed just a furrow long,
Man drove his oxen.
Gladly he sang a simple ploughman's song
Of crops hard-earned.

Over rich fields the plough-shares carve their ways;
Man drives the tractor.
In sweet forgetfulness of former days
The soil is turned.

But as of old the thoughtful man stops now,
To pray once more that God will speed the plough.

1964

A Man Who Loved Trees

Beyond the east window cascades a laburnum,
Yellow flowers trembling in the cool breeze;
The lilac is fragrant, the copper beech glowing,
As we say farewell to a man who loved trees.

Soft notes from the organ, from bowed heads a murmur;
Over the countryside sounds the sad bell.
But out in the woodlands a cuckoo is calling
Its message of May to the trees he knew well.

Many he planted, and long they'll outlive him,
Sycamores, chestnuts, now thronging with bees.
But surely they'll welcome in heavenly gardens
The spirit of William, a man who loved trees.

(On May 29th, 1965, William Cottrell was buried at Sall, Norfolk.)

The Garden Gate

In His own image, from the earth,
God made a man. Man proves his worth
When in his turn he can create
Such beauty in a garden gate.

A web of gossamer inspired
The skilful craftsman who aspired
To mould the metal and produce
This masterpiece for daily use.

And those who pass along this lane
Will pause, and think, and think again...
If man, with stubborn iron, does work so fine,
What will God do with man, with skill divine?

1967

(The wrought iron gate, in the form of a spider's web,
was made by Eric Stevenson, of Wroxham, Norfolk.)

Eggs for Tea

When Granny gives us eggs for tea,
Oh, what a treat! It seems to me
There cannot be a better sight
Than eggs in egg-cups, boiled just right.

And I must say I like them most
Beside a round of buttered toast,
Cut up in 'soldiers'; they look great
All lined up there upon my plate.

And if I can't take off the shell,
My Grandad does it very well;
He wears his spectacles, you see;
They help a lot, it seems to me.

I give my egg a careful poke,
And find the lovely, golden yolk.
Sometimes it pops outside the cup,
But Granny quickly cleans it up.

My tasty soldiers I start dipping,
And up they come again, all dripping
With lovely egg, and then I eat 'em!
They're so delicious; you can't beat 'em!

At last I see the shell so brown
With nothing left; so upside down
I turn it in my egg-cup then
And wish that it was full again.

(Written for the grandchildren, 1984.)

Pooh Sticks

Sometimes we go to Itteringham
It's not too far away;
We find a little wooden bridge,
A special game to play.

We get a lot of Pooh sticks,
(Named after 'Winnie-the-Pooh')
And one by one we throw them
In the water down below.

And then we wait and watch for them
To come again in view;
Though some get stuck beneath the bridge,
Most of them travel through.

They twist and turn and wander
Along the River Bure;
They have a thrilling journey,
Of that I'm very sure!

If I was very little
On my Pooh stick I'd ride
Down river right to Yarmouth,
And go out with the tide.

I'd be a proper sailor,
And have a lot of fun,
And sit and eat bananas
On an island in the sun.

(Written for the grandchildren, 1984.)

Look Yew Up!

We caan't show yew a mount'n,
An' bor, we're short o' hills;
An' yew oon't taake long a-countin'
Ar caastles an' ar mills.

But don't yew set there sighin';
Jus' caast yar oyes up high
Where clouds an baads're flyin',
An' see ar Norfolk sky!

1973

Cawston Chaach Tower

Five hunnerd year tha's stood there, that gret tower,
A-lookin' down at what go on below,
As one by one the generaations pass,
Times chaange, an' other buildin's come an' go.

That fare t'point the way t'laastin' things
Wha's far away above the grassy sod;
By night, the mune an' stars in that wide sky,
By day, the sun an' clouds, an' always... God.

1970

New Year Resolutions

Taake care what yew dew, an taake care what yew're sayin';
Taake time when yew're trav'lin', an'more when yew're prayin'.
Dew yew keep on smilin', an' if yer like, sing;
A laaugh dew yer good, an' that don't corst a thing!
Don't yew overdew it when eatin' or drinkin',
An' whatever yew dew dew, yew leave time fer thinkin'!

1971

78

The Little White Rabbit

That died today,
That little white rabbit,
An' she set there an' cried.
That were her own,
Her pet, that rabbit;
She loved it; then that died.

Poor little mawther,
She's on'y saven.
In't naathin' yew can say.
Tha's allus haard
T'laarn, y'know...
God give; God taake away.

1970

Poem for Conservation Year, 1970

They'a bin an' cut a new rud where the ole rud useter run,
An' there in't no corners no more.
They'a lavelled out that hill where Jimma hed'is mill,
Tha's as flat as a pancaake, bor!

They'a felled that line o' poplars what were seen fer miles around;
They were lovela in the mornin' light;;
An' there in't a bush na' tree where the spinney useter be,
Dew yer know, that don't seem right.

The Jolly Farmers pub has gone, an not a stun in't left,
An' tha's a rea' long walk ter the Crown
An' that little kissin' gaate where the mawthers useter wait,
O' course tha's bin took down.

The blackbaads an' the maavishes hin't got nowhere ter go;
There in't a nestin' plaace in sight,
An' each day yew see a-lyin' little creatures, dead or dyin',
Cut down by cars at night....

Them cars what go a-roarin' paast at sixta mile an hour –
They call that progress, I suppose.
But then tha's allus plain, whenever someone gain,
There's allus someone else what hatta lose.

1970

Contentment

A warm June evenin', a-gardenin'; a lark in the sky;
Earth on m'hands; a kitten a-playin' nearby;
House-martins burblin', clingin' there high on the wall;
Sweet peas, an' pansies, an' carrots, an' celery an' all.

Scent o' the pinks, an' the roses; an yew settin' there
Runnin' orf honey, like amber. I reckon, m'dear
We'a got the bes' things; that don't matter much about money,
Trew love, peace o' mind, all them flars... an jus' look at that honey!

Mary's Birthday, 1970

Susan's Weddin'

The ches'nuts got their can'les
Alight an' bright an' new;
There's May-flars on the hedges,
An' the taaters're all t'rew.
The bees're on the blossom,
An' the cuckoo call away,
Ah, the warld that seem right merry
On Susan's weddin' day.

The people draw along t'chaach,
They come from far an' wide;
An' there's others at the winders
What wanter see the bride.
The p'leeceman he's right busy tew,
Wi' motors by the score,
An' there in't no sarvin' in ar shop,
They're crowdin' roun' the door.

We're all dolled up right proper,
An' the chaach, why, tha's a wonder,
Tha's packed right out wi' people
Like that never is a Sunda'.
There's some what set there smilin',
An' others set an' sigh,
An' here an' there a mother
Quietly hev a little cry.

At laast the weddin's over;
We all go on ar way.
Fer all o' us I reckon
Tha's bin a lovela day.
We'a drunk the health o' bride an' groom,
We'a hed ar photies took...
There'll be some happy mem'ries, bor,
In Susan's weddin' book.

23rd May, 1970

Here Come the Combine

Here come the combine, cuttin' t'rew the barley,
See the crop a-fallin' as on that run,
Roun' an' roun' the fild there, carvin' out a pathway
O' prickly ole stubble, dusty in the sun.

Handy on the hidlan' there's a traailer a-waitin',
Wi' rich gold grain pilin' up right high.
Here come the baaler, gath'rin' up the straw now,
Tidyin' up the fild tha's a-clankin' by.

A few hours pass an' the fild's right empty,
The combine travel on its way, that dew;
An' orf up the rood go a load o' barley,
Fust load o' haarvest, an' a good one tew!

1979

84

Fairy Taales

In my young days, when children found
A ring o' toodstules on the ground,
The old'uns allus useter say,
'That's where the fairies dance at night.'
An' wide us littl'uns' eyes would grow,
An' more an' more we'd wanter know
'Bout where the fairies went by day,
An' wonder if that could be right...

An' if on some ole wayside tree
A toodstule like a seat we see,
We'd sune be told, 'On them there things
The pixies sit, this time o'year.'
I haard them taales long years ago,
Yit still I like t'think, y'know,
Of fairies daancin' in them rings,
An' little pixies settin' there...

1979

The Ole Orchard

Tha's many a year ago, that is,
Since ole Tom say t'me, he say,
'I reckon as I'll hev suffin' new –
I'll hev an orchard!' An' he set tew,
An' not tew far from his cottage door
He staarted a-puttin' in fruit trees, bor.

I mind right well when they fust did fla'r,
An' how he shewed 'em t'me wi' pride.
He'd trouble wi' frorst an' bugs an' baads,
An' time an' agin he'd use strong waads,
But he cared fer them, an' them trees growed tall,
Apples an' pears an' plums an' all.

Yew'd never believe the fruit what come
From that little ole orchard down the laane.
Come each September they'd hang b'the score,
Green an' yaller an' red – why, bor,
They looked a pitcher as yew passed there,
An' Tom see evraone hed a share.

That seemed right fittin' that he should die
When them trees were laaden like never afore.
'Corse times ha' chaanged, an' his cottage ha' gone,
But that ole orchard o' his go on,
Apple an' plum an' tall pear tree –
What better memorial could there be?

1979

Autumn Shadders

Autumn wear on, an' the shadders come suner
Over the filds when the sun sink low;
Shadders o' tall trees lay 'crorss the medder,
Poplars an' willers, like giants in a row.

Shorter the days now an' culer the evenin's,
An' haardly a sound of a baad kin yew hear.
Then out come the stars, an' a paale mune t'foller,
Bringin' a whisper o' frorst in the air.

Here come an owl flyin' out o' the spinney,
Sorft wings outspread, like a ghoost he dew pass.
Naathin' alse move in the magic o' munelight;
Mune shadders lay on the silvery grass.

1979

Pore Ole Toad

There he lay, that pore ole toad...
He hatta crorss this busy rood,
Like toads ha' done for many a year,
T'reach that pit jus' over there.
Come spring they hatta up an' go
T'find the water there below,
So's they can lay their eggs an' see
Them little tadpools swimmin' free.
Their best paace, that in't very faast,
Though they done o' right in the paast,
But nowadays, wi' all this speed,
They jus' han't got the skill they need
T'dodge the cars, bor, like they ought.
Why, even hoppin' toads git caught,
An' lay there flattened, like them others,
This here ole toad, his sisters, brothers,
An' all them creatures what ha' need
T'crorss the rood so's they can breed...
I'm sorry they git all this worry
Corse we're in such a flarin' hurry.

1979

The Blackbaad's Nest

There they be, t'ree on 'em, brown-speckled, lovely,
Clus in the nest in the hawthorn jus' there,
Near where the holly tree stand in the hedgerow;
Look at them eggs, bor, the fust o' the year.

Up there above set the ole faather blackbaad,
Lookin' right smaart wi' his yaller beak tew;
Here come his wife; tew the nest she's retarnin' –
Sune that there pair'll hev plenty t'dew!

Tha's one o' the miracles goin' on round us,
One o'them things took fer granted each day.
But in each o' them eggs – dew yew jus' think about it –
The song of a blackbaad is all stored away.

1979

The Ind o' the Year

The ind o' the year ha' come today,
Another milestun on the way.
Time don't haalf fly; that never stay,
   Somehow.

An' tha's a rum'un, tew, y'know,
That as us old'uns older grow
Ole Faather Time he quicker go
   I vow!

The paast tha's gone; that in't no more.
The future on'y God know, bor.
The time fer dewin', tha's fer shore,
   is now!

1979